Welcome to Busy Book 3!

These things are hidden in this book. Can you find them? Write the page number in the circle.

 parrot

 skateboard

 pirate

 dragon

 camera

 paintbrush

 banana

 ice cream

 fish

 monkey

 trainers

 mountain

The Busy Book helps children develop in the following areas of learning...

 Communication
Learning to speak together in English.

 Leadership
Learning to build relationships.

 Discovery
Building knowledge and awareness of social responsibility.

 Critical thinking
Solving problems and puzzles and learning thinking skills.

 Creativity
Expressing ideas through drawing and making.

 Self-management
Learning to plan ahead to reach goals.

1 All about school!

Circle six differences in these two pictures.

a

b

Sort these school words.

More FUN
How many blue books are in the pictures?
_____

notebook

paint

crayon

Art	Maths

paintbrush

pen

ruler

Imagine with Alicia

Goldilocks and the Three Bears

What do you do every day? I'm Goldilocks and this is my morning.

I wake up at seven o'clock.

I have a shower.

I have breakfast.
I love porridge!

I brush my teeth.

I go to school.

Goodbye Baby Bear, Mum Bear and Dad Bear!

Colour the bowls to match. Retell the story to a friend.

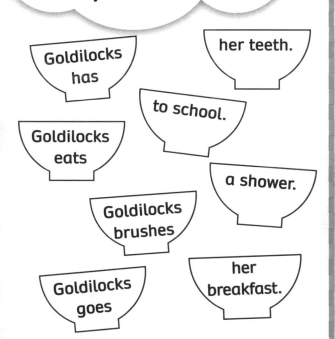

Goldilocks has

her teeth.

to school.

Goldilocks eats

a shower.

Goldilocks brushes

Goldilocks goes

her breakfast.

About me

I wake up at _____.

I have _____.

I brush _____.

I go _____.

3

Questionnaire

Circle for you and tick for a friend or family member.

Would you rather...?

 get up at **six o'clock** or eight o'clock?

go to school every day or only on Mondays?

wear a **school uniform** or your own clothes?

have lessons inside or outside?

learn **Art** or Science?

have **a pool** or **a trampoline** at school?

have a fish or a hamster for a class pet?

wear shoes or trainers?

have **sandwiches** or **ice cream** for lunch at school?

Think of two more questions. Then ask a friend or family member.

Riddle

I've got four legs but I can't walk. What am I?

_____

4

Our world

Look and write the subjects.

PE   Science   Drama

1 I like _____.   2 I like _____.   3 I like _____.

Astronauts are good at Science, Maths, ICT and PE!

Find out more

What are the most popular jobs in your country?

5

Design a classroom

Draw your perfect classroom and write.

Use ideas from the box or choose your own.

outside   inside   desks   chairs
paintbrushes   garden   posters   blue walls
board games   paintbrushes   class pet

Is it inside or outside?

_____

What is in your classroom?

_____

_____

Ask and answer with a friend.

Is your classroom inside or outside?

It's outside. It's great!

Read and tick or write.

Things I like in this unit:

The puzzle ☐

The story ☐

_____

Things I am good at:

Writing about my day ☐

Creating my perfect classroom ☐

_____

Explore our town!

Help Leo and Poppy find the places.

START

FINISH

Find and write the six places Leo and Poppy go to.

More FUN

Where's Spud the dog?

_____

_____   _____

_____   _____

_____   _____

My town

Look, read and answer.

This is my town, I like my town.
Ask and answer with me.
Is there a **pharmacy**?
Yes, there is.
Is there a **supermarket**?
No, there isn't.
Is there a **police station**?
_____

Are there any **shops**?
Yes, there are.
Are there any **beaches**?
_____

Are the people kind
and **friendly**?
_____

Change the words to make true sentences.

There isn't a pharmacy.
There is a supermarket.
There aren't any shops.
There is a beach.

What is the town square in Ryan's town like?

It's big. ✓ ✗   It's small. ✓ ✗

It's old. ✓ ✗   It's new. ✓ ✗

FUN FACT

The smallest town in the world is called Hum, in Croatia. Only 30 people live there!

Guessing game

Choose a word and draw it for your friend to guess.

beach	librarian	bus	shop assistant
bus driver	café	village	police officer
friendly	doctor	big	bus stop
city	hospital	car	supermarket
sports centre	waiter	town	cinema

Tell me a joke!

What kind of city is dangerous?

Electri**city**!

Our world

Rearrange the letters to write the places.

1

2

3

wton

itcy

ellgvia

_____ _____ _____

Write.

A _____ is small. There aren't lots of people.

Some _____ have got small shops.

A _____ has got more people. There are schools, supermarkets, and sometimes a sports centre or a cinema.

A _____ is very big. There are lots of people and there are hospitals, libraries and lots of shops and cars.

Find out more

What is the biggest city in the world?

Do you live in a village, a town or a city? Go outside and look around. Draw and write about what you can see, hear and smell.

About me

I live in a _____.

I can see _____.

I can hear _____.

I can smell _____.

Design a city

Design a city of the future. Draw and write.

My city of the future

There's a _____ in my city.

It's got a lot of _____ .

There are some _____ .

There isn't a _____ .

There aren't any _____ .

You can cut out pictures from magazines to use in your design.

Show your picture to a friend or a family member. Tell them about your city of the future.

Read and tick or write.

Things I like in this unit:

The puzzle ☐

The game ☐

_____

Things I am good at:

Writing about where I live ☐

Designing a city of the future ☐

_____

Look at the picture and complete the puzzle.

School play rehearsal today

More FUN

How many things starting with 's' can you find?

_____

Alfie's Storybook

Read the story. Find and write the hidden words.

I've got a book.

It's an amazing storybook.

I want to show you my book.

Look at my book!

There's a princess and a dragon.

The princess is _____!

The dragon is _____!

This story is about pirates. They have got a map. They are looking for treasure.

The pirates are _____.

Good luck, pirates!

The giant is big and _____.

Help! She's in my room!

Oh – it's OK. The giant is

_____. What an adventure!

About me ★

I like stories about _____ and

_____.

I don't like stories about _____.

More FUN

Think. What's in the giant's basket?

_____

Guessing game

pirate giant monster
spy superhero dragon
astronaut prince princess

Draw these things in the blank squares. Don't tell your friend.

	1	2	3	4
a	(book)			(star)
b			(robot)	
c	(treasure map)			(photo)
d	(parrot)		(horse)	

Play the game with a friend.

Is there a pirate in A3?

No, there isn't.

Is there a giant?

Yes, there is.

Read and match.

Do you want to become an author?
Read this guide. How many things can you do?

How to become an author

1 **Write a diary**
Write a diary every day! Always make time to write. Then it is part of your routine!

2 **Write about something you know**
Write a story about your pet dog's day or write about your favourite hobby.

3 **Read a lot!**
Read newspapers and magazines. Visit a library and try some new books!

4 **Read your work aloud**
When you write, read your work aloud to a friend or someone in your family. Ask their opinion. Listen to their ideas to help with your story!

Good luck!

a

b

c

d

Find out more

What famous story characters are there from your country? What are they like?

A famous storybook character from

my country is _____.

He / She is _____ and

_____.

FUN FACT The first storybooks for children are from Japan. They are 800 years old!

Create a character

Draw and write about a storybook character. Choose words to help or your own words.

giant   princess   prince   spy
superhero   astronaut   pirate

scary   dark   cute   long   clever
short   brave   kind   fair   strong

T-shirt   rabbit   dress   dragon   turtle
jumper   belt   frog   cap   monster

dragons   books   monsters
ice cream   football

Here is my amazing storybook character.

He / She is a / an _____ . His / Her name is

_____ . He / She is from _____ .

He / She is very _____ but he / she isn't

_____ . He / She has got _____

hair. He / She always wears a very big _____

and a red _____ . His / Her best friend is a

_____ . He / She likes _____ .

He / She doesn't like _____ .

Show your character to a friend or someone in your family. Tell them about your character.

Read and tick or write.

Things I like in this unit:

The crossword ☐

Learning about books ☐

Things I am good at:

Playing the game ☐

Writing about a storybook character ☐

_____   _____

Imagine with Alicia

Summer camp

Find the words in the frame. Then read and write the words.

vtrtrghilactinpentbzdeoutsideeae

pctinskcomputerbakcardscasportq

utsxtkuinstrumentbzdeoideg

It's summer camp.
My favourite camp!
It's fun to be busy with my friends.

We can learn an ____________.
I'm learning the guitar!
We can play ____________ games.
My friend likes swapping ____________.

Draw your own activity.

It's summer camp.
My favourite camp!
It's fun to learn something with my friends.

We can ____________, read books and play.
We like being ____________, too.

We do ____________ and jump and run.
What do **you** want to do?

Which activities do they do at summer camp? ✔ or ✘

FUN FACT

The boy in the picture is doing origami. Origami is a type of paper craft from Japan. The wings of the largest origami bird ever made were almost 82 metres long!

Hobbies survey

Do a survey. Ask your friends and family.

Find someone who ...

likes being outside
name: _____
name: _____
name: _____

likes doing crafts
name: _____
name: _____
name: _____

likes helping people
name: _____
name: _____
name: _____

is good at playing an instrument
name: _____
name: _____
name: _____

wants to learn coding
name: _____
name: _____
name: _____

likes learning something new
name: _____
name: _____
name: _____

likes taking photos
name: _____
name: _____
name: _____

is good at acting
name: _____
name: _____
name: _____

Do you like being outside?

Yes, I do. I love being outside.

Riddle

? A cat has got three. A girl has got four. What are they? ?

_____

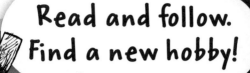

Read and follow. Find a new hobby!

Hobby finder

No — Do you want to be outside? — Yes

Do you want to be with friends? No

Do you want to stay at home?

Yes

Yes

Do you like doing crafts?

Do you like sports?

No

Yes

Yes No Yes No

Do you like games?

Do you want to be with friends?

Yes No **3** **4** **5** **6** Yes No

1 **2** **7** **8**

1 play computer games
2 try acting
3 try knitting
4 learn an instrument
5 play badminton
6 take photos in the garden
7 go to the cinema
8 go swimming

CINEMA

Why is it a good idea to try new hobbies?

Two things I like doing:

_____

_____

Two new things I want to try:

_____

_____

How I feel about trying new things: _____

_____

Plan a party

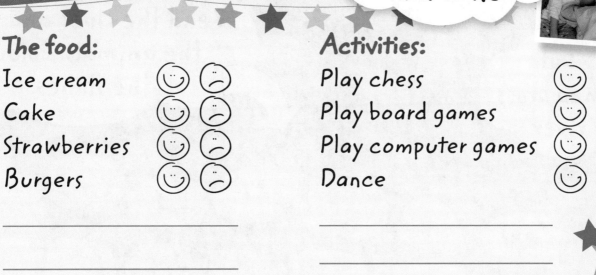

Think about your party. Circle and write.

The food:

Ice cream 🙂 🙁

Cake 🙂 🙁

Strawberries 🙂 🙁

Burgers 🙂 🙁

_____

_____

Activities:

Play chess 🙂 🙁

Play board games 🙂 🙁

Play computer games 🙂 🙁

Dance 🙂 🙁

_____

_____

My friends: _____

Find out more

What are traditional party games in your country? What about in other countries?

Now write your invitation.

You are invited to _____'s party!

Date: _____ Time: _____

Please bring: _____

Read and tick or write.

Things I like in this unit:

The survey ☐

Learning about new hobbies ☐

_____

Things I am good at:

Reading in English ☐

Planning a party ☐

_____

21

5 Let's save our animals!

CLUES

1 I'm black and white. I can't run fast.

2 I can run. I've got spots.

3 I live in trees but I can't fly.

4 I am very big. I haven't got fur.

5 I'm a bird but I can't fly.

6 I've got stripes but I'm not black and white.

7 I can't run but I can fly.

8 I am long. I haven't got legs.

More FUN
How many things starting with 't' can you find in the picture?
_____

The lion and the mouse

Read the story.

What does the lion say at the end? Imagine and write.

Deep in the jungle, there's a lion. He's sleeping. Be careful, little mouse!

I can see you, little mouse!

Now, the lion isn't sleeping...

The lion is big, but he's kind.

I can see a lion! It's big! Be quiet!

Help! I can't run!

Ok, you can go free little mouse.

The next day, the lion is walking in the jungle.

The mouse is small, but she's brave!

Help me, please!

I can help you. You're my friend now.

FUN FACT

Lion cubs (babies) have got spots when they are born. Later, they lose their spots.

What is the message of the story?

Tell the story to a friend or someone in your family.

Imagine and draw your own jungle. What animals live there?

Compare with a friend.

Is there a leopard in your picture?

No, there isn't. But there are two lions. They've got fur.

Tell me a joke!

What kind of key opens a banana?

A mon**key**!

Our world

Look and write.

1 deer

2 birds

3 squirrels

_____ are grey or red. You can see them in your street or your garden. They can climb trees.

There are lots of _____ in the city. They can fly into your garden.

_____ are big animals. They sometimes come into the city.

About me

This is my favourite animal.

It's a/an _____.

It lives in _____.

Find out more

What animals live in your neighbourhood? Go outside and look. Draw and write.

I can see _____.

There are lots of _____.

There aren't any _____.

Design an animal

Imagine a new animal and label it.

Has it got spots or stripes?

Can it fly?

Has it got a tail, feathers or wings?

How many legs has it got?

Ask and answer with a friend.

Has your animal got stripes?

No, it hasn't. But it can fly.

Read and tick or write.

Things I like in this unit:

Cross the River game ☐

Learning about animals in my neighbourhood ☐

_____

Things I am good at:

Naming animals in English ☐

Designing an animal ☐

_____

Come on an adventure!

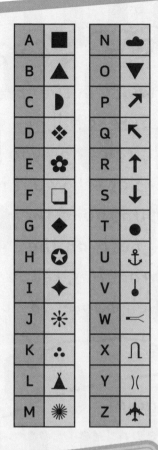

A	■	N	☁
B	▲	O	▼
C	◗	P	↗
D	❖	Q	↖
E	✿	R	↑
F	▢	S	↓
G	◆	T	●
H	✪	U	⚓
I	◆	V	♦
J	✹	W	✄
K	∴	X	∩
L	▲	Y	)(
M	✳	Z	✈

Isabel

Olly

Use the code. Find the activities.

Ryan

William

Ruby

Isabel is ↓ ∴ ■ ● ✿ ▲ ▼ ■ ↑ ❖ ◆ ☁ ◆ .

_____.

Olly is ↑ ▼ ◗ ∴ - ◗ ▲ ◆ ✳ ▲ ◆ ☁ ◆ .

_____.

Ryan is ◗)(◗ ▲ ◆ ☁ ☁ ◆ .

_____.

William is ✪ ■ ♦ ◆ ☁ ◆   ■   ↗ ◆ ◗ ☁ ◆ ◗ .

_____.

Ruby is ▲ ⚓ ◆ ▲ ❖ ◆ ☁ ◆   ■   ❖ ✿ ☁ .

_____.

Draw you and a friend doing an activity.

Write a message to your friend in code.

_____

_____

_____

More FUN

How many squares are in the codes above?

_____

27

Shape poems

Read.

Big
And old.
Green in the
summer and white in
the **winter**. I can see a tiny hut.
The **mountain** is beautiful.

It is **windy** in the **forest**.
But the **tree** is tall and **strong**.
How many circles can you see on it?
The circles tell you it is old.
Birds build their
nests on the
branches, ready
for their babies to come.

On the **island**, everything is quiet.
The sun shines. It is hot and sandy here on the **beach**.
I like fishing in the **sea** and listening to the sea singing to me.

Write a river poem.

~~~~~~~~~~~~~~~~~~~~
~~~~~~~~~~~~~~~~~~~~
~~~~~~~~~~~~~~~~~~~~

About me

Places that I like in the countryside:

_____

_____

Activities that I like doing in
the countryside:

_____

_____

Activities survey

Ask your friends and family. Tick. Then write.

What's your favourite activity for...

a sunny day?

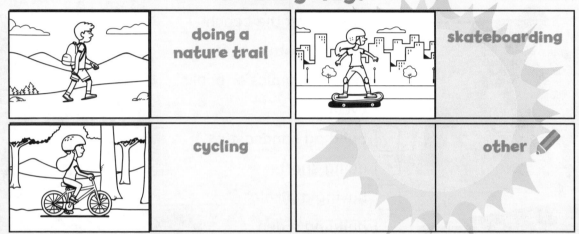

	doing a nature trail		skateboarding
	cycling		other ✏️

a rainy day?

	reading		playing board games
	doing crafts		other ✏️

Tongue twister

Can you say this quickly five times?

The six quick kids are fishing in the forest.

The most popular activity for a sunny day is

_____.

The most popular activity for a rainy day is

_____.

29

Our world

What activities do you like doing on holiday? Tick.

- [ ] playing on the beach
- [ ] doing a nature trail
- [ ] reading comics or books
- [ ] cycling
- [ ] building sandcastles
- [ ] doing sports
- [ ] having a picnic
- [ ] building a den
- [ ] sailing
- [ ] doing crafts

Find out more

What is a famous holiday place in your country?

FUN FACT

The tallest sandcastle in the world was made in Germany. It was nearly 18 metres tall!

Summer journal

Write and draw.

My favourite places in the summer are...

_____

My favourite things about summer are...

_____

My favourite summer activities are...

_____

This summer, I would like to...

_____

Show your journal to a friend or someone in your family. Tell them about it.

Read and tick or write.

Things I like in this unit:

The code puzzle ☐

Learning about holiday activities ☐

_____

Things I am good at:

Writing short poems ☐

Asking questions in English ☐

_____

 **Goodbye**

About me

I like this book because...

_____

_____

The best thing in this book is...

_____

_____

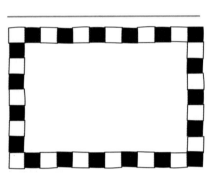

Something I learnt in this book is...

_____

_____

Rise and Shine Certificate

You finished Busy Book 3!

Well done!

Awarded to: _____

Age: _____ Date: _____

Thomas
Thomas

Alicia
Alicia

Daniel
Daniel

Rafa
Rafa

Lena
Lena